HOW TO DRAW
CUTE STUFF

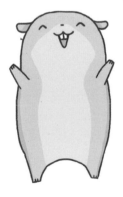

HOW TO DRAW
CUTE STUFF

Angela Nguyen

STERLING CHILDREN'S BOOKS
New York

CONTENTS

STERLING CHILDREN'S BOOKS
New York

An Imprint of Sterling Publishing Co., Inc.

ISBN 978-1-4549-2564-4

Distributed in Canada by
Sterling Publishing Co., Inc.
c/o Canadian Manda Group,
664 Annette Street,
Toronto, Ontario,
Canada M6S 2C8

For information about custom editions,
special sales, and premium and
corporate purchases, please contact
Sterling Special Sales at
800-805-5489 or
specialsales@sterlingpublishing.com.

Conceived, edited, and designed by
Quarto Publishing plc
6 Blundell Street
London N7 9BH

Manufactured in China

Lot #

18 20 19

www.sterlingpublishing.com

Hi there,
my name is Angela!

I'm an artist who specializes in drawing cute stuff. Anything small, fluffy, or with a face, you can count on me! For as long as I can remember, I've always had the urge to draw cute things. An empty whiteboard is a calling to draw something, anything! An open sketchbook is an opportunity to sneak a cute note to the owner!

One of the reasons I like to draw is the mysterious phenomenon that cute illustrations always make people happy. Even if it is just a small doodle on somcone's napkin, it never ceases to brighten a person's day. It also can't be helped when cute things are all around us. We find them in animals, like dogs, and places, such as our own homes. We find them in the activities we enjoy and the people we love.

In this book, I've illustrated a collection of cute people, animals, and objects that are a big part of my life. Whether you're a beginner or the best artist in your group of friends, why not join me and learn how to draw cute stuff, too?

Angela Nguyen

Chapter One

GETTING STARTED

You don't need any special tools or materials to start drawing cute stuff. Experiment with different pens, pencils, and surfaces, and learn how to give subjects cute appeal!

TOOLS AND SURFACES

My usual tools include a black marker,
my sketchbook, my laptop, and my tablet.

Metallics
add sparkle!

Use art markers for
rich color and vibrancy.

There's no going
back with a pen.

Colored pencils are
great for shading.

Be bold with
a marker.

The pencil
is a go-to!

Clean up with
an eraser!

Sharpies
define lines.

Anything can become a drawing surface! Take this leaf, for example.

Use a sketchbook to keep all your drawings in one place. Don't have a sketchbook? A simple notebook will do.

Sticky notes are fun to draw on. You can stick them anywhere and everywhere!

TECHNIQUES FOR CUTIES

Anyone can draw cute things with these simple guidelines.

1 Let's begin by drawing some basic shapes; a circle, triangle, and square. Nothing cute about them, just a bunch of shapes.

2 Now try drawing the same three shapes, but this time with rounded corners. Which looks more cute, the sharp or the rounded shapes?

3 Give your rounded shapes a face. Now your simple shapes have been transformed into cute shapes! All you need for cuteness is roundness and faces.

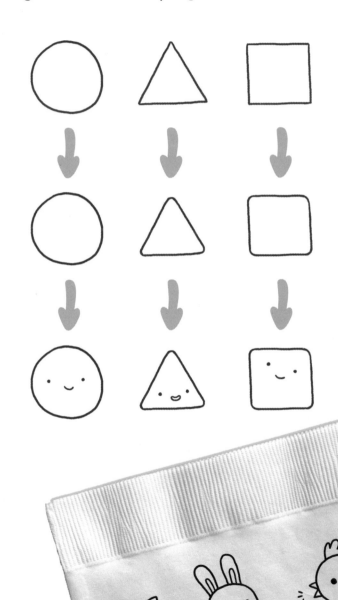

EYES

Cute eyes can be achieved with a simple dot or line. You can scribble in the dots to give a "sparkle" effect.

NOSE AND MOUTH

Add a small nose for a punch of cuteness. Draw a round mouth and perhaps a cheeky tongue!

COLORS

Pastel colors are always cute. Try to find light colors for extra cuteness!

SHADOWS

Shadows give your drawings dimension. Consider where your light is coming from. Areas near the light source are paler and those further away are darker.

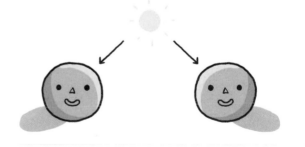

EFFECTS

Sparkles, flowers, hearts, and blushing always make your drawings cuter.

HOW TO MAKE EVERYTHING CUTE

The main four things to remember when drawing cute things are:
1 Simplify, **2** light colors, **3** roundness, and **4** faces.

1 Simplify and use less detail.

This way, the drawing can focus on being cute! Focus on simple shapes and take out the details to make cute drawings.

2 Light colors complement simple drawings.

I like to use pastel colors rather than bright, intense ones.

3 Roundness helps to soften drawings.

Taking away sharp features and adding roundness to your drawings makes them cuter. There's just something about that small and chubby look…

Use round shapes in place of sharp corners.

4 Adding a cute face is the ultimate secret!

Transform anything you want into something cute by drawing on a face.

Look at my keyboard's cute face. We love to have jam sessions.

PROPS MAKE PERSONALITIES

Props can give your characters more personality. People can have items like clothing or jewelry. Even animals can have accessories.

1 This is just a simple dog. But I added extras transform it.

2 Add a backpack and now it is an adventurous dog!

3 Add sparkles and now it is a fabulous dog!

MOTION

Adding lines help to show the motion of your drawings.

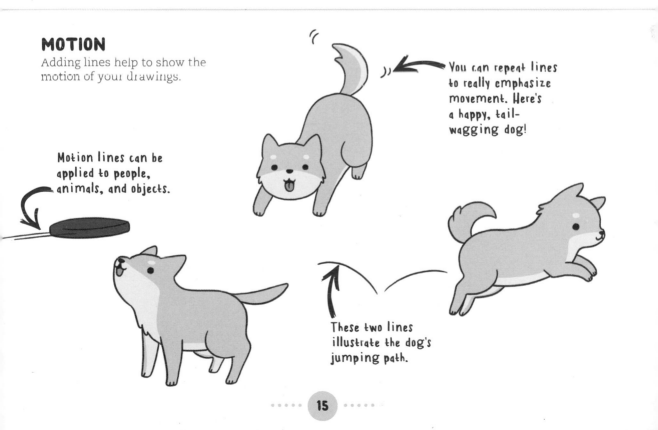

You can repeat lines to really emphasize movement. Here's a happy, tail-wagging dog!

Motion lines can be applied to people, animals, and objects.

These two lines illustrate the dog's jumping path.

Chapter Two

CUTE PEOPLE

Drawing cute people requires features to distinguish them, and accessories and clothes to decorate them. In this chapter, I'll show you how to bring all sorts of characters to life!

PROPORTIONS

Two-and-a-half circles make a basic figure.

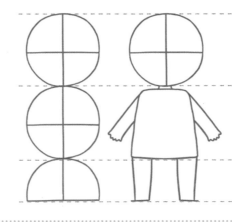

PERSPECTIVE

I like to use horizontal and vertical lines to help me draw people turned in different directions. The horizontal line is where the eyes and nose rest. The vertical line is the center of the person's face.

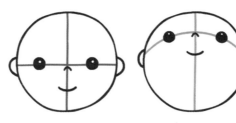

If you draw the horizontal line higher, your person will be looking up.

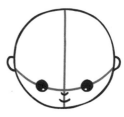

Move the horizontal line lower and your person will be looking down.

HAIRSTYLES

There are so many different hairstyles you can give your character. Hairstyles can also make your person look more like a boy or a girl.

Put some clothes on and
then you've got a person.

You can add eyelashes to make
your person more feminine.

If you draw the
vertical line to the
left, your person will
be looking left.

Move the vertical
line to the right and
your person will be
looking right.

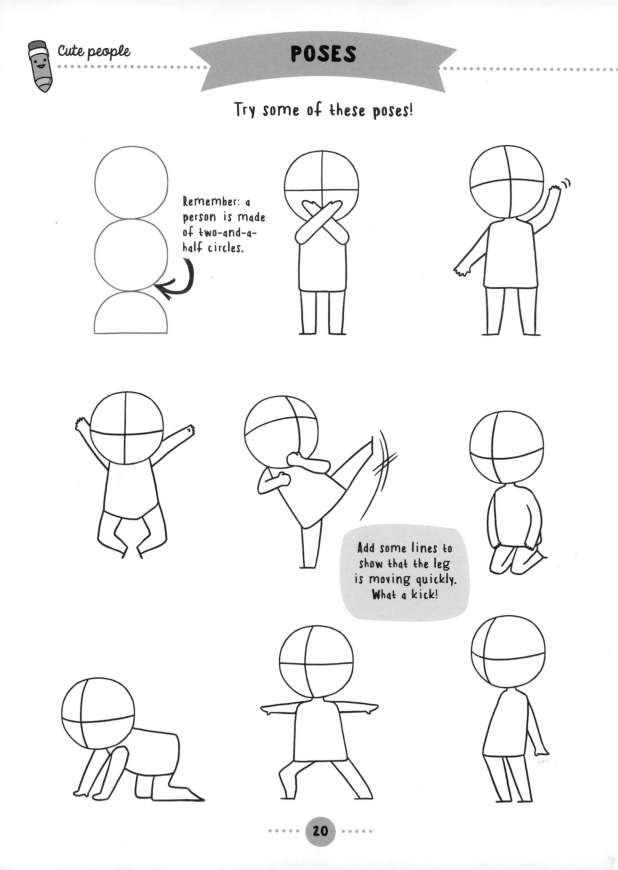

POSES

Try some of these poses!

Remember: a person is made of two-and-a-half circles.

Add some lines to show that the leg is moving quickly. What a kick!

I can balance on one leg.

Raise the horizontal guideline on your character's face to make them look up.

Changing the angle of the feet can help with the gesture. Try making your person tiptoe.

EXPRESSIONS

What mood is your character in?

NEUTRAL

HAPPY

I call these
"smiling eyes."

ANNOYED

CONFUSED

WORRIED

Draw some lines
on the side of the
face to add to the
expression.

DISGUSTED

EXCITED

One of my favorite
symbols is sparkles.

SAD

Eyebrows can help
emphasize an
expression.

ANGRY

The eyebrows are
so expressive!

SCARED

Add chills around
the face for a more
spooky effect.

FULL

SICK

Add eye bags to exaggerate the eyes.

EMBARRASSED

Add some blush.

Symbols like a water drop can make your person look guiltier.

GUILTY

LOVE

You can always change the shape of your person's eyes.

SMIRK

SHOCK

Jagged lines and an open jaw is the key to this expression.

CRYING

Watery eyes and a watery waterfall.

TIRED

A cloud coming out of the mouth looks like a big sigh.

SLEEPY

TOPS

Now that you know the basics of drawing a person,
you can dress them up in different ways.

A T-shirt is a simple top.
You can add a little pocket
to spice things up.

A strapless dress is easy to
draw; just remove the sleeves!

Changing the shape
of the edge of a shirt can
change the entire mood.

A belt can be a nice touch to a dress.

Keep your character warm by giving them a long-sleeve sweater.

If you draw a T-shirt and cut off the sleeves, you get a cut-off shirt.

Combine and layer tops to create sets.

By changing the collar of a T-shirt, you can get different kinds of shirts, like this V-neck.

Add a cute cat graphic, too.

BOTTOMS

There are so many different styles of bottoms you can draw to dress your character. Here are just a few to choose from.

Anything can go with jeans.

Sweat pants are baggy and have soft edges.

These are even baggier!

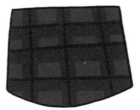

There are so many patterns that can be applied to clothing. Try this polka-dot print.

Draw jagged patches for ripped pants.

Adding an extra fold can transform your skirt.

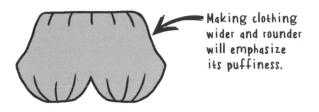

Making clothing wider and rounder will emphasize its puffiness.

Don't be afraid to try asymmetry, too!

Draw a matching top to complete your pajamas.

You can explore different kinds of pants just by changing the edges.

I love drawing plant graphics.

Overalls can wrap over your top.

HATS

Fuzzy hats are fun
to draw and wear.

Head accessories don't have
to cover the whole head.

This is how I keep
my head warm in
the winter.

GLASSES

You can change the size of your glasses to be small or big.

The horizontal guidelines on your character's face are super helpful for drawing glasses.

Some glasses have one lense and go across the whole face.

Don't forget that you can change the shape, too.

BAGS

A tote bag can be held or placed over one shoulder.

A messenger bag is drawn across the body, like the side bag.

Strings for straps? Must be a drawstring.

Here's what a backpack looks like on.Two straps go over the body.

JEWELRY

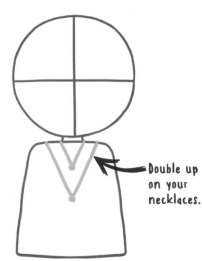

Double up on your necklaces.

A small necklace around the neck can make a nice accessory.

Drawing the same shapes over and over can create a necklace pattern, like this flower lei and triangle necklace.

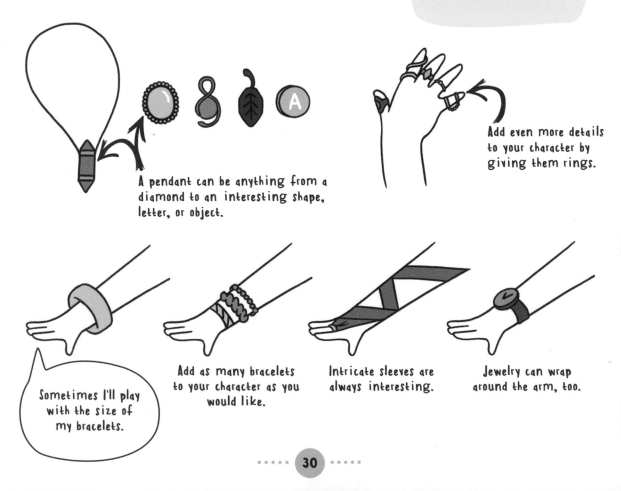

A pendant can be anything from a diamond to an interesting shape, letter, or object.

Add even more details to your character by giving them rings.

Sometimes I'll play with the size of my bracelets.

Add as many bracelets to your character as you would like.

Intricate sleeves are always interesting.

Jewelry can wrap around the arm, too.

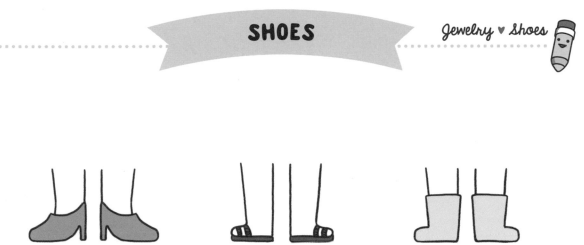

The key to drawing high heels is to angle your feet.

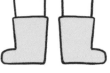

Boots rise higher on the legs than sneakers.

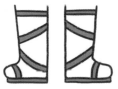

Even complicated shoes with multiple straps can be easily drawn over your sketch.

Bunny shoes can have faces, too.

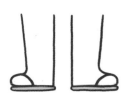

Shoes can be drawn on top of your character's feet. These sneakers fit perfectly over the sketch.

POLICE

Match outfits and add accessories to complete your character!

Deck your character out with an equipment belt and cool shades.

The smirking face can be accompanied by the crossed-arms pose.

Draw a running pose to show her chasing after the criminals.

She can't resist donuts! Look at those heart eyes.

ASTRONAUT

Astronauts have slightly bigger heads because of their helmets.

The helmet can also hide your astronaut's face.

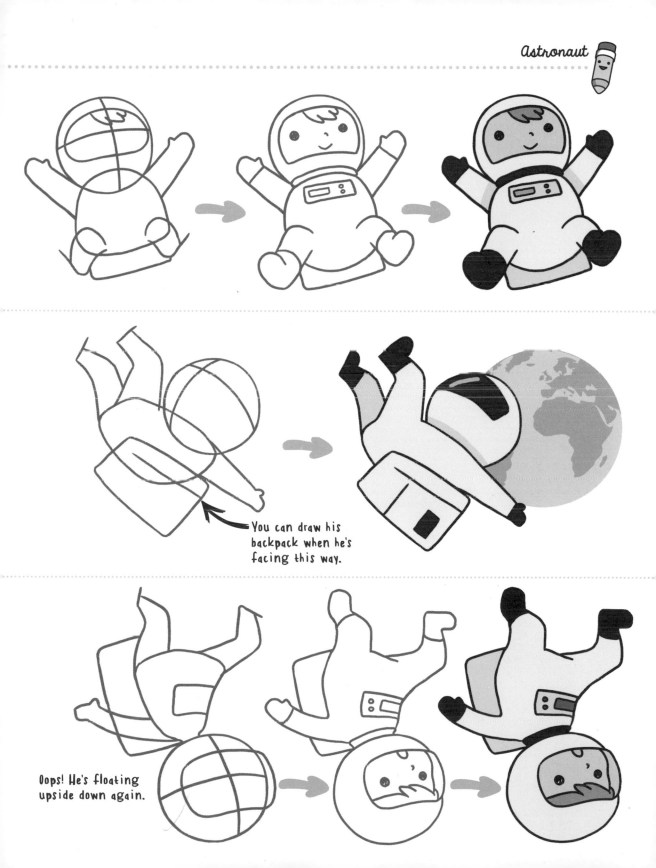

Astronaut

You can draw his backpack when he's facing this way.

Oops! He's floating upside down again.

CHEF

Your chef can have a short apron or a long one.

The dish is perfect!

Draw wavy lines coming from the plate to show the delicious scent.

Master chef is a master egg flipper! Add lines from the pan to the egg for movement.

COWBOY

Adding eyebrows gives me more character.

Cowboys are so cool! This expression can be drawn with closed eyes and a smirky smile.

Did you know that cowboys herd cattle?

COWGIRL

Cowboy ♥ Cowgirl

The cowgirl and her lasso can be drawn with ovals.

Yee-haw! Draw jagged symbols to indicate movement.

Oh, no! Cowgirl has been tied up by Cowboy.

DOCTOR & NURSE

Give your doctor a stethoscope so he can check heartbeats.

Ouch! Sharp! Nurses have to be careful with their gear.

This coat has a lot of pockets to hold notes and pens.

Add symbols near the face for a surprised effect.

FARMER

Yum! Add a bite mark to the apple the farmer is eating.

Your farmer is a hard worker. The sweat drop and expression say it all.

Keep the crops growing! Give your farmer a watering can.

NINJA

Draw your ninja right-side up and then turn your paper upside down.

Your ninja can do a high kick if you make him or her lean back.

Give your ninja stars to throw.

Ninja punch! Draw lines to represent speed and movement.

When climbing, you can hang your ninja's weapon on his or her back.

43

SAILOR

Draw your sailor in a pointing pose.

Is that land?

The sailor salutes the captain.

Give your sailor a telescope so he can see farther.

X marks the spot.

You can draw your own treasure map.

WITCH

You can make a cute witch by giving her a big hat and a simple dress.

A successful potion! Draw a green aroma coming out of the glass.

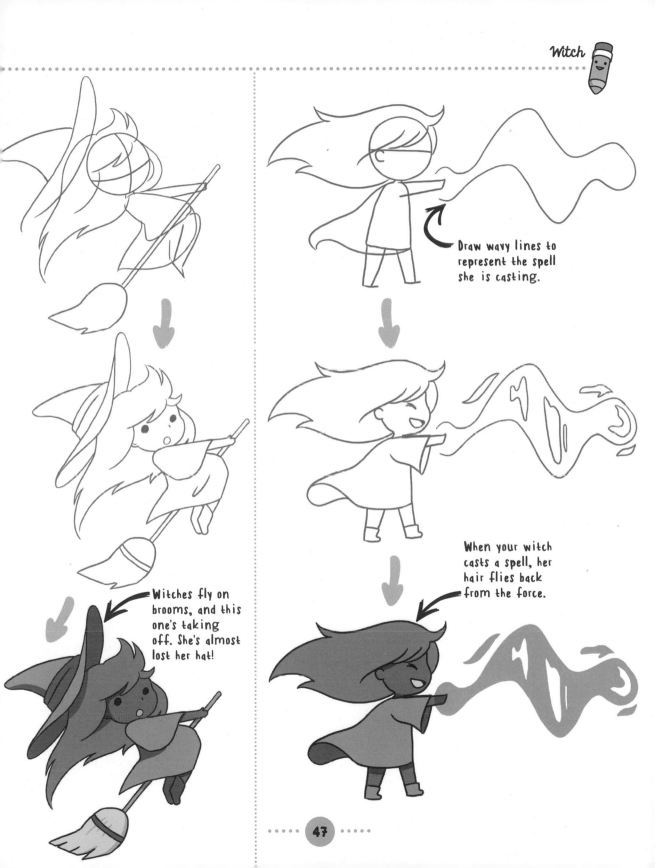

Draw wavy lines to represent the spell she is casting.

When your witch casts a spell, her hair flies back from the force.

Witches fly on brooms, and this one's taking off. She's almost lost her hat!

Chapter Three

CUTE CREATURES

From dogs and cats to mythical creatures and even insects, this chapter shows you how to make every animal extra cute!

DOG

Dogs are so loyal and loving.

Play fetch with your dog and draw it jumping.

Some dogs are hairier than others. Look how fluffy this dog is!

Make your dog's fur flow in the wind when it runs.

Dog

Look at how the dog's legs move.

Check out this dog's wrinkly forehead!

Curl up your dog when it sleeps.

Z Z Z

CAT

I'm similar to a dog, but a bit more round in shape.

You can make your cat fluffy by giving it more hair.

Draw a little tongue for your grooming cat.

Cats are very playful!

RABBIT

Cat ♥ Rabbit

Rabbits are made of three main circles.

Rabbits can stand on their feet when sniffing something.

Droop your rabbit's ears when it is sleeping.

ELEPHANT

Elephants are mostly made of circles.

Use two shades of gray to add three dimensionality.

Tuck the trunk under the sleeping elephant's head.

Eyebrows and steam puffs make an angry elephant.

The elephant is scared! Curl its trunk and draw the ears folded back.

Draw tear drops and droopy ears for a sad elephant.

You can accessorize your elephant. Start with a bow tie under its mouth.

The rear of an elephant is made from three simple circles.

To give your elephant an object to hold, draw its trunk curled around it.

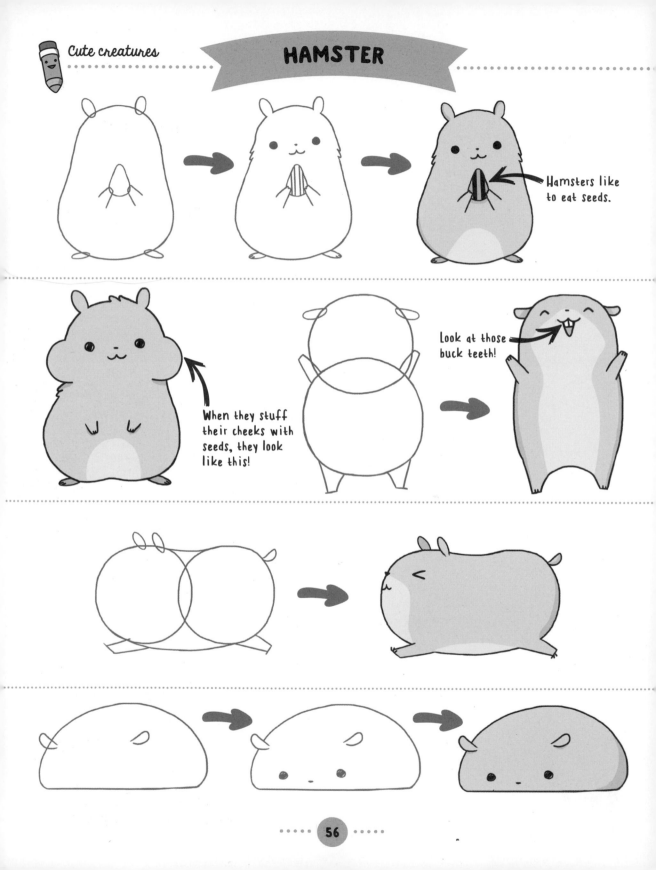

HAMSTER

Hamsters like to eat seeds.

When they stuff their cheeks with seeds, they look like this!

Look at those buck teeth!

Squirrels have really fluffy tails.

Try drawing this climbing squirrel on a tree.

Drawing a chipmunk is similar to a squirrel, but make the tail less fluffy.

BEAR

Bears are drawn with big circles and paws.

Bears get really big when they stand!

Color your bear white and it becomes a polar bear.

Pandas have black arms, legs, ears, and eyes.

58

DEER

Bear ♥ Deer

Add spots to your deer's back.

When drawing deer, notice how long their legs are.

Sometimes deer stand up to get food from low trees.

Simple lines can become intricate antlers.

FOX

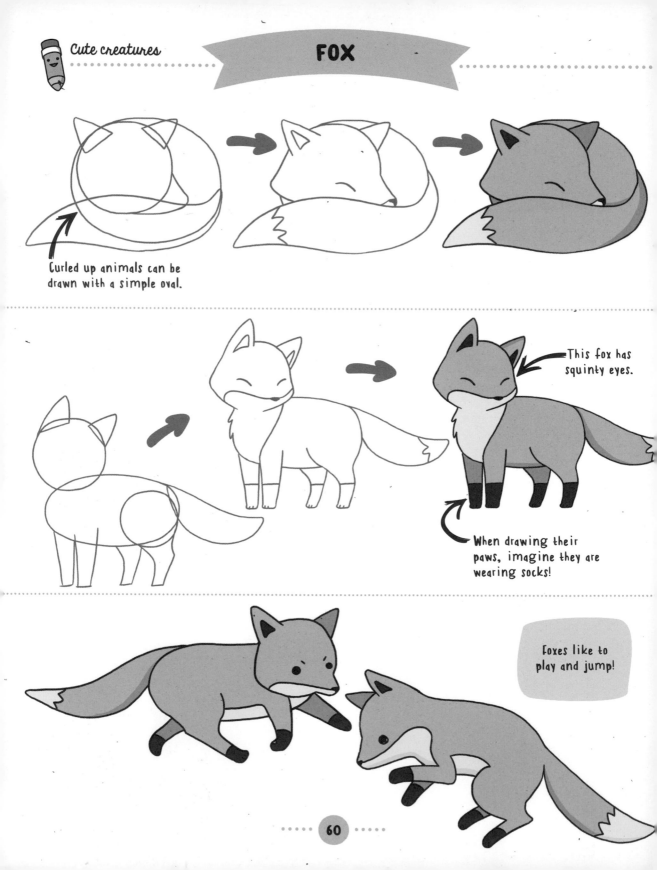

Curled up animals can be drawn with a simple oval.

This fox has squinty eyes.

When drawing their paws, imagine they are wearing socks!

Foxes like to play and jump!

RACCOON

Raccoons have stripy tails.

What is this raccoon reaching for?

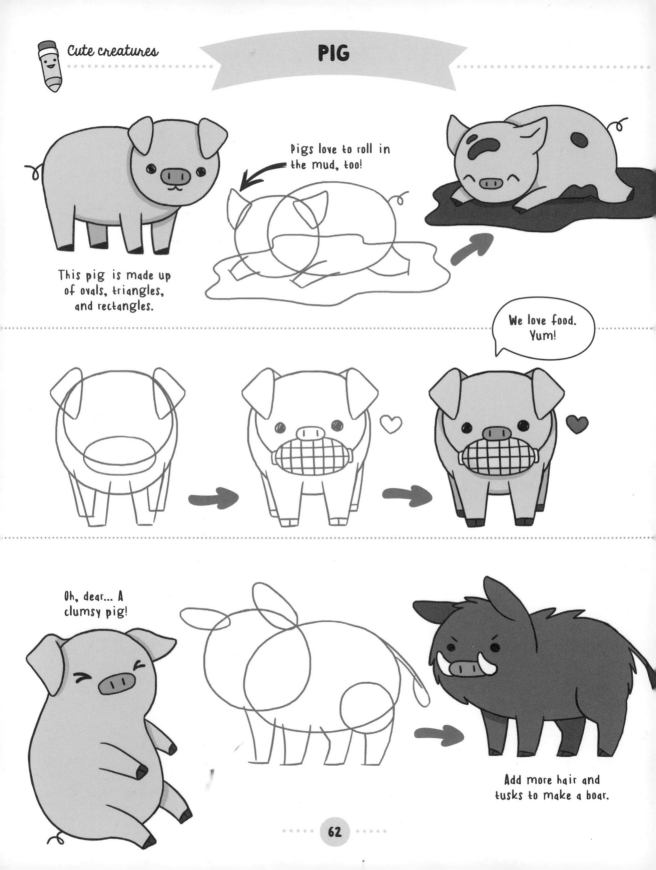

PIG

Pigs love to roll in the mud, too!

This pig is made up of ovals, triangles, and rectangles.

We love food. Yum!

Oh, dear... A clumsy pig!

Add more hair and tusks to make a boar.

Pig ♥ Turtle

Turtles bring their houses with them.

A tortoise is a larger turtle!

Here's a turtle going as fast as he can!

Draw a hexagon to get the shell shape.

Sea turtles have rounded arms and pointed shells.

KOALA

Koalas have big noses.

Aww, look at the baby koala.

Koalas like to cling to things, like trees.

Draw a happy expression for this koala!

Koalas always seem to be laying around, but don't forget they crawl, too.

MONKEY

Draw two circles when starting your monkey.

Some monkeys are fuzzy and have small tails.

You can draw one arm up to create a hanging monkey.

Draw thicker arms and you've got yourself a gorilla!

LION

Drawing a lion's head requires two circles: one for the face and one for the mane.

Make your lion roar loudly by drawing a big, open mouth!

TIGER

A tiger's pattern may look complicated, but it is just a repetition of stripes!

Try to space the tiger's stripes out evenly so they don't look clustered.

Do you think the tiger or the lion would roar louder?

Tuck the front paws in between the legs when the tiger is running.

GIRAFFE

A giraffe's pattern is like a puzzle that doesn't connect!

A giraffe from the front looks silly!

Did you know giraffe's tongues are purple?

ALLIGATOR & CROCODILE

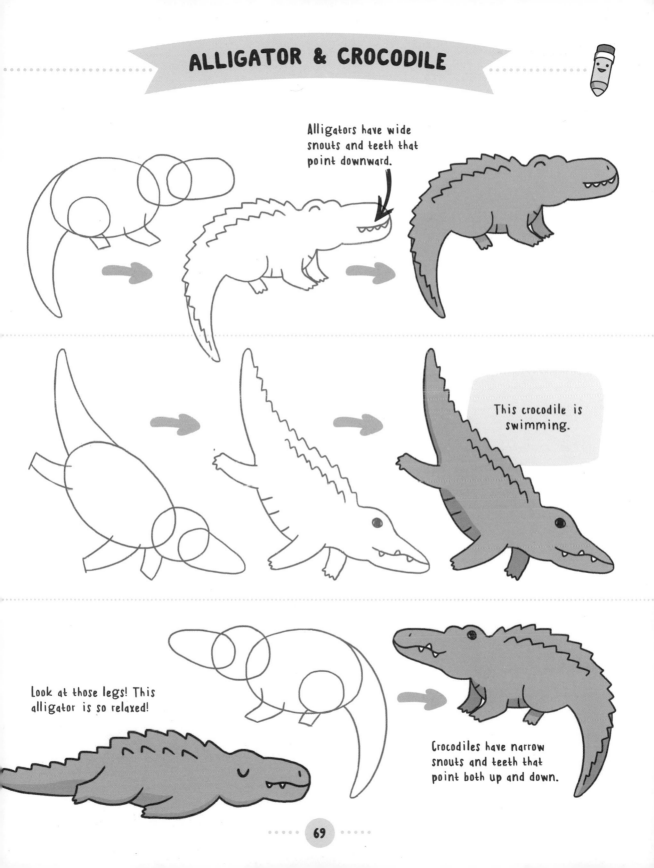

Alligators have wide snouts and teeth that point downward.

This crocodile is swimming.

Look at those legs! This alligator is so relaxed!

Crocodiles have narrow snouts and teeth that point both up and down.

COLORFUL BIRDS

Did you know flamingos are only pink because of what they eat?

Draw lines by the wings to show that hummingbirds fly very fast.

Colorful birds

If you make your bird plump, it will be so adorable!

Kiwis can be brown or white.

Parakeets have patterns around their eyes.

Parrots can come in all kinds of colors, including bright green and yellow!

Draw a big beak for a toucan.

CITY BIRDS

Look at those eyes.

Color your bird black and it becomes a crow.

Sparrows can be super fluffy.

Seagulls can be found in urban areas by bodies of water.

DUCKS

Ducks have funny patterns around their necks.

Ducklings can be drawn with two circles.

Some ducks have cool hairstyles.

Open up your duck's wings to let it fly!

FLIGHTLESS BIRDS

Ostrich are too big to fly!

Don't make an ostrich angry!

Baby penguins are fuzzier than adult penguins.

Penguins like to slide on their bellies.

Eagles have fluffy necks.

Eyebrows show that this hawk means business.

This hawk is clenching its fist!

These wings are large and powerful.

OWL

Eyebrows can change an owl's expression.

Some birds can be drawn with one circle.

If you draw a circle for the owl's head and body, it looks like it's flying toward you.

BAT

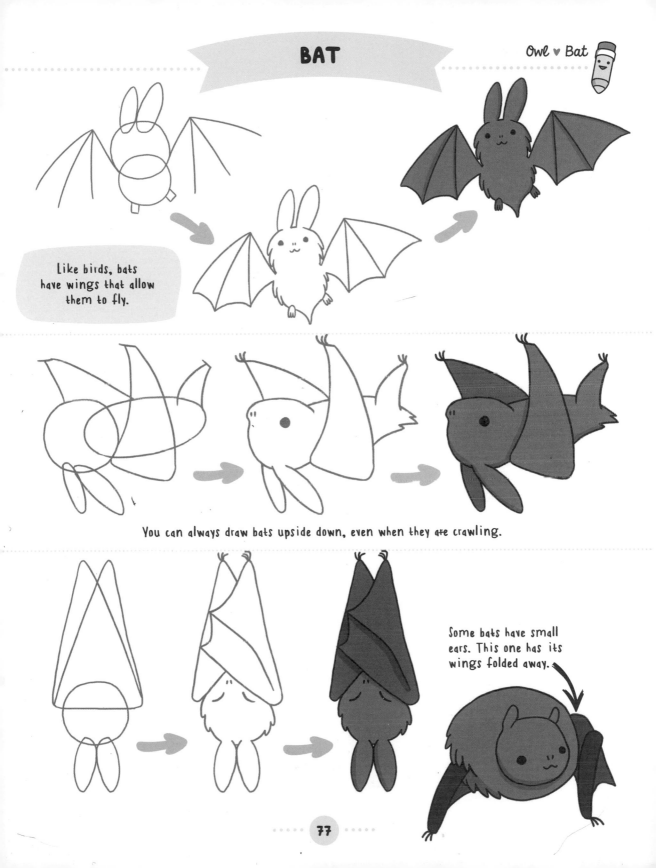

Like birds, bats have wings that allow them to fly.

You can always draw bats upside down, even when they are crawling.

Some bats have small ears. This one has its wings folded away.

COLORFUL FISH

Clownfish are orange and white.

Some salmon can be really colorful!

Draw a heart to make this fish.

A goldfish can be drawn with one circle.

Draw a big circle for a puffed-up puffer fish!

Draw a small oval for an un-puffed puffer fish.

Draw long fins to make an angelfish.

Not only is this fish colorful, it also has patterns!

DOLPHIN

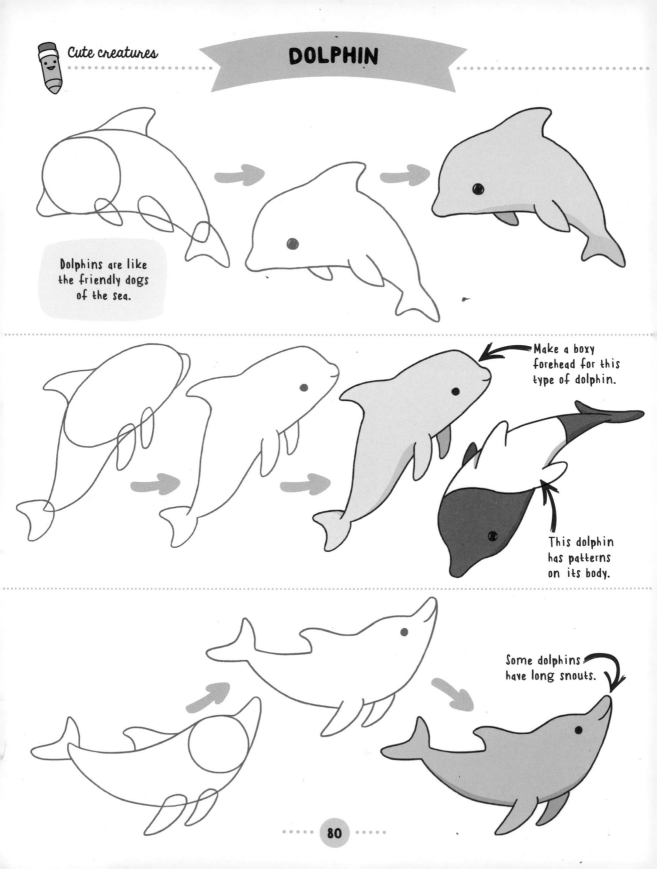

Dolphins are like the friendly dogs of the sea.

Make a boxy forehead for this type of dolphin.

This dolphin has patterns on its body.

Some dolphins have long snouts.

Dolphin ♥ Shark

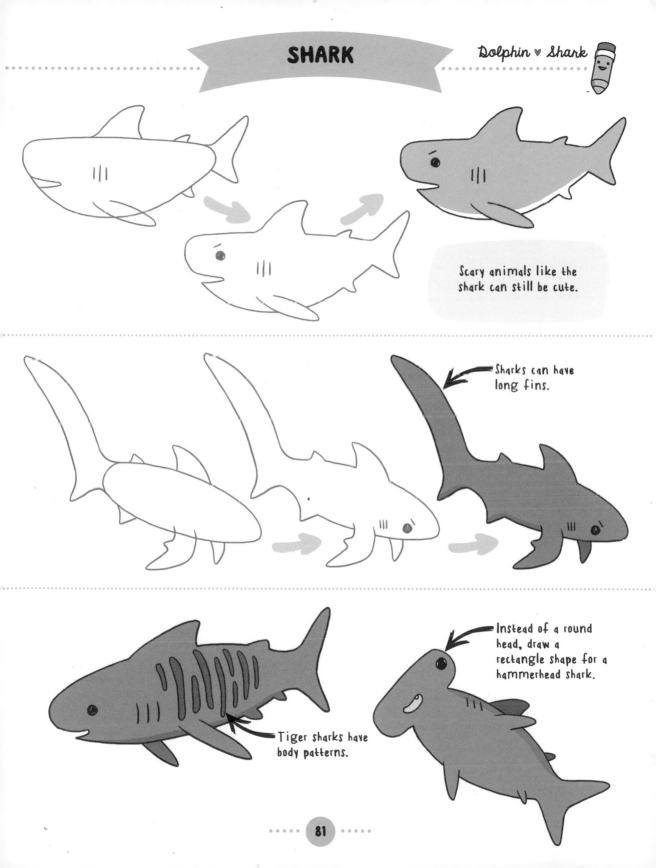

Scary animals like the shark can still be cute.

Sharks can have long fins.

Tiger sharks have body patterns.

Instead of a round head, draw a rectangle shape for a hammerhead shark.

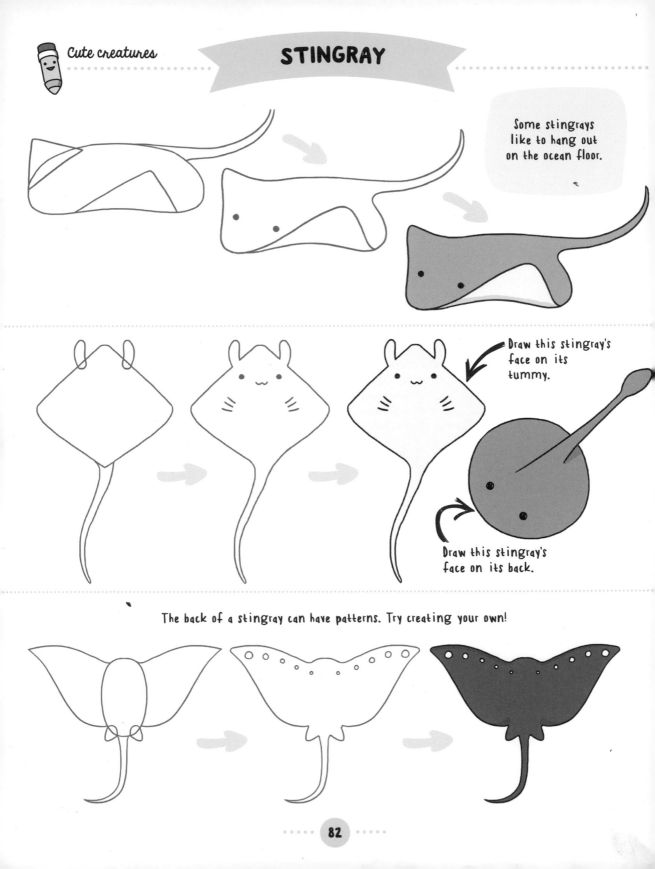

STINGRAY

Some stingrays like to hang out on the ocean floor.

Draw this stingray's face on its tummy.

Draw this stingray's face on its back.

The back of a stingray can have patterns. Try creating your own!

Whales are the largest animals in the sea.

Some whales have large foreheads.

Killer whales are similar in shape to dolphins.

TENTACLES

Draw lines for jellyfish tentacles because they are very skinny.

Draw the face on the shell or the body for different looks.

Squid have little legs and long arms.

Some octopuses have flat arms.

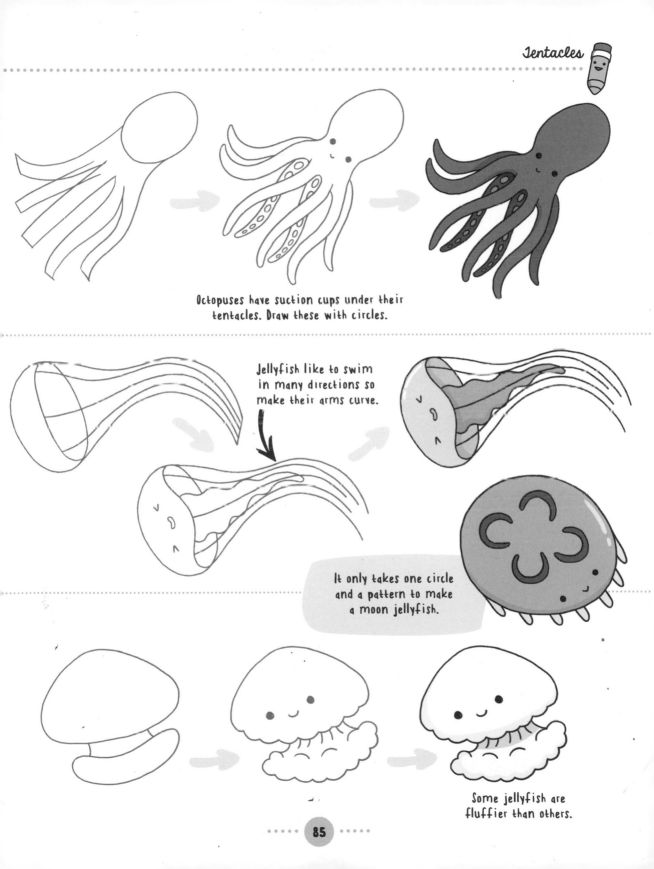

Octopuses have suction cups under their tentacles. Draw these with circles.

Jellyfish like to swim in many directions so make their arms curve.

It only takes one circle and a pattern to make a moon jellyfish.

Some jellyfish are fluffier than others.

CATERPILLAR

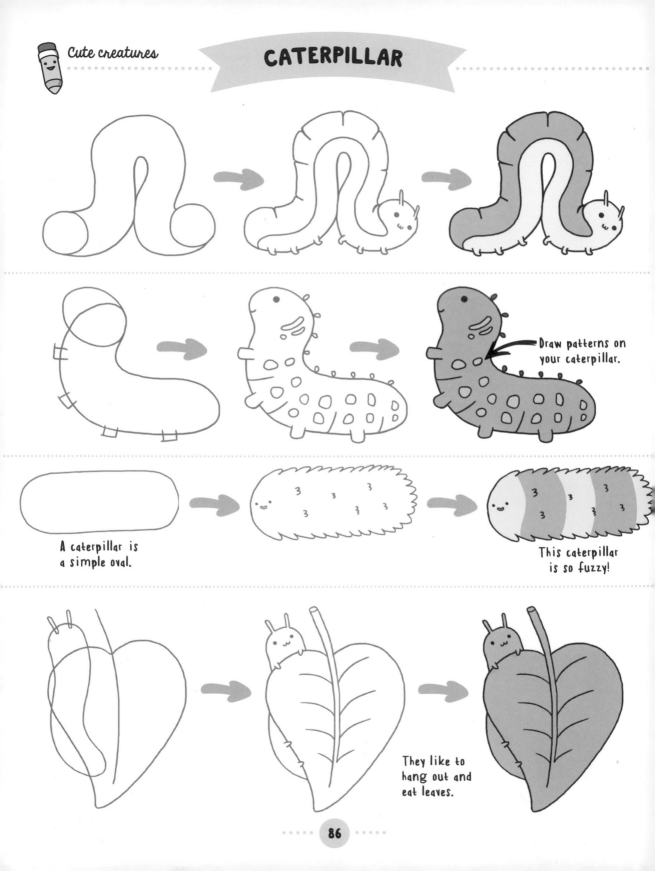

A caterpillar is a simple oval.

This caterpillar is so fuzzy!

Draw patterns on your caterpillar.

They like to hang out and eat leaves.

BUTTERFLY & MOTH

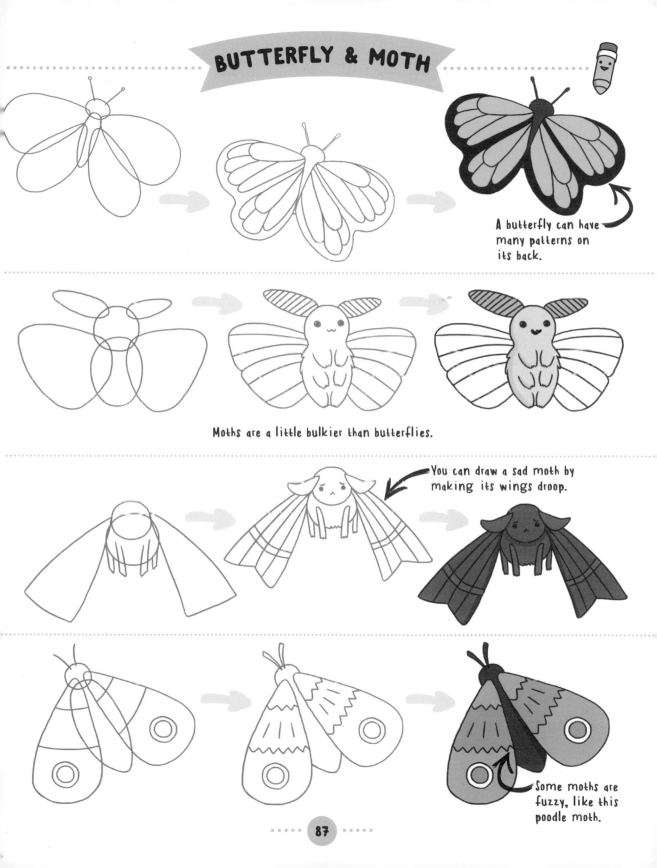

A butterfly can have many patterns on its back.

Moths are a little bulkier than butterflies.

You can draw a sad moth by making its wings droop.

Some moths are fuzzy, like this poodle moth.

GRASSHOPPER

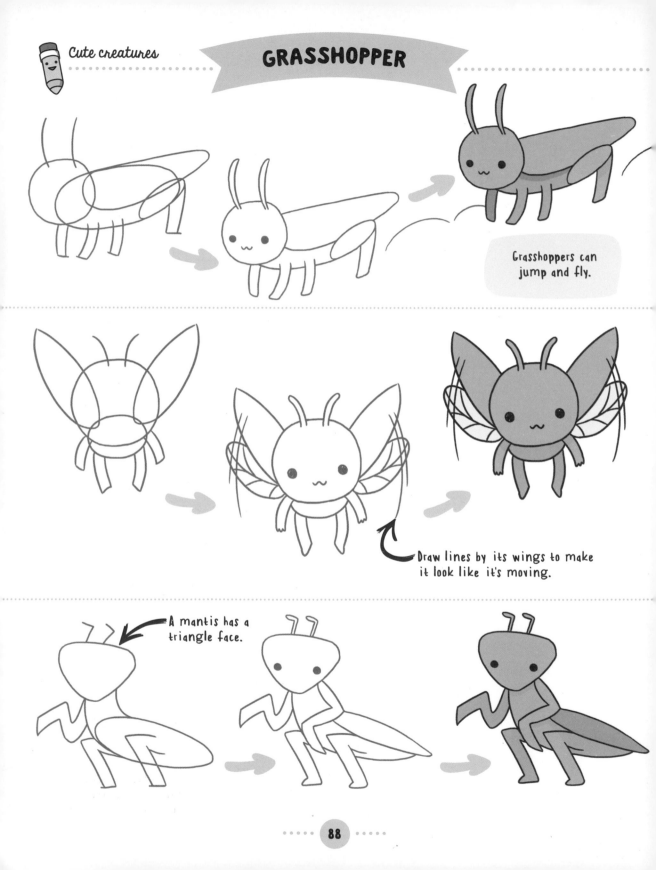

Grasshoppers can jump and fly.

Draw lines by its wings to make it look like it's moving.

A mantis has a triangle face.

LADYBUG

Different ladybugs have different patterns.
Try to come up with your own.

A flying ladybug!

This ladybug doesn't
have spots on its back,
but does on its face.

BEE

Bees have fuzzy necks.

You can draw a stinger on your bee to make it look fierce.

Beehives are a bunch of connecting hexagons.

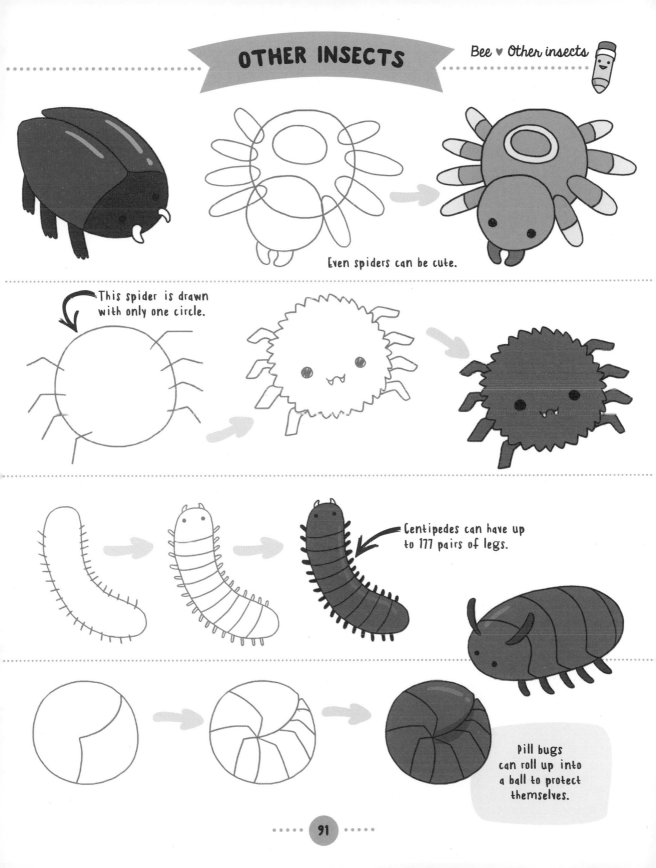

Even spiders can be cute.

This spider is drawn with only one circle.

Centipedes can have up to 177 pairs of legs.

Pill bugs can roll up into a ball to protect themselves.

Cute creatures

DRAGON

Dragons are giant reptiles that breathe fire.

This dragon is on all fours.

You can make your dragon stand.

Dragons curl up when they sleep.

Dragon

Some dragons have two heads.

Add spikes to the spine of your dragon.

A dragon without limbs is a serpent.

UNICORN & PEGASUS

A unicorn is a horse with a horn.

A pegasus is a horse with wings!

Spread your pegasus's wings to let it fly.

Phoenix have long and beautiful tails.

The trick to making a phoenix different from a regular bird is to add wavy feathers.

Add eyebrows to your phoenix to give it some spunk.

LOCH NESS MONSTER

My nickname is Nessie.

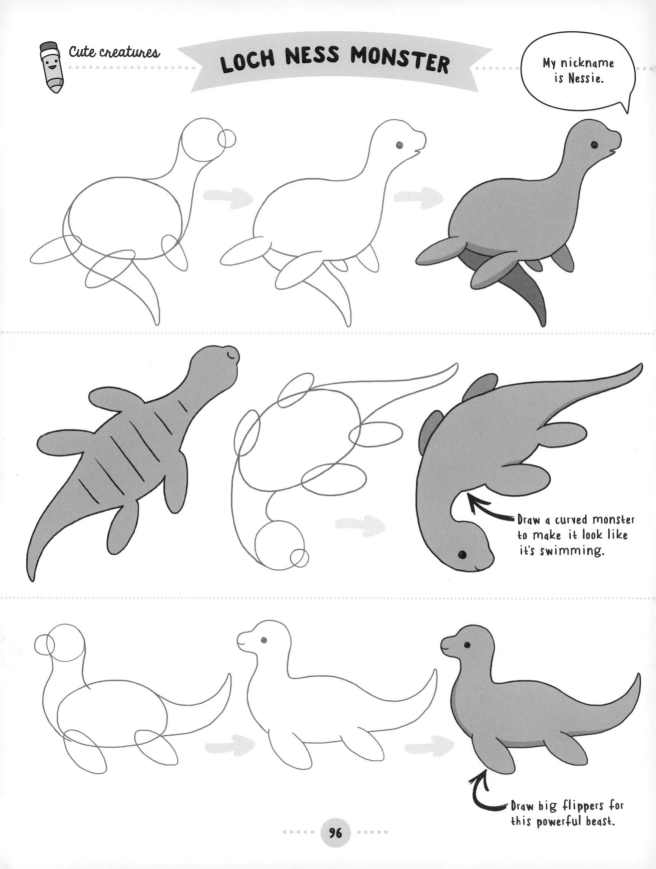

Draw a curved monster to make it look like it's swimming.

Draw big flippers for this powerful beast.

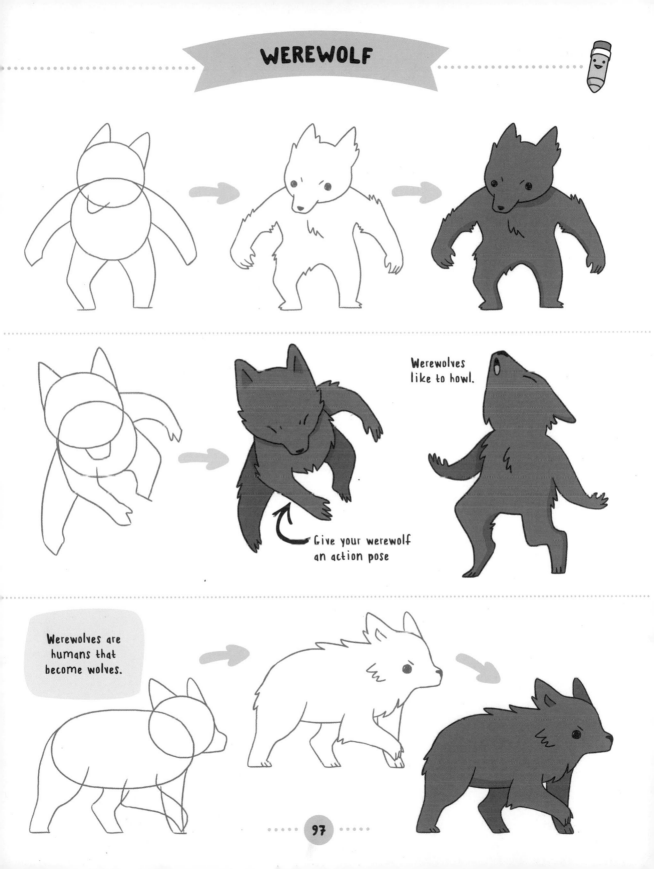

Werewolves like to howl.

Give your werewolf an action pose

Werewolves are humans that become wolves.

Chapter Four

CUTE THINGS

Everything can be cute! This chapter focuses on inanimate objects, from chairs to cooking tools and everything in between!

BUILDINGS

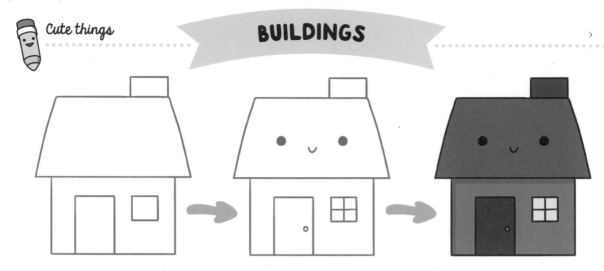

Look how cute your home can be by just adding a face.

Draw a home for your farm animals.

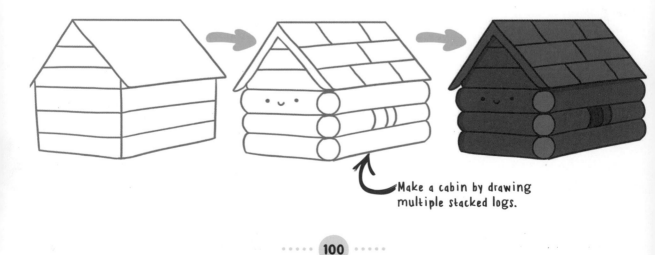

Make a cabin by drawing
multiple stacked logs.

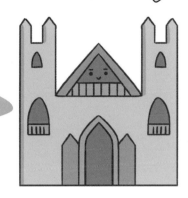

Cathedrals are large buildings.

A greenhouse is where you can keep your plants.

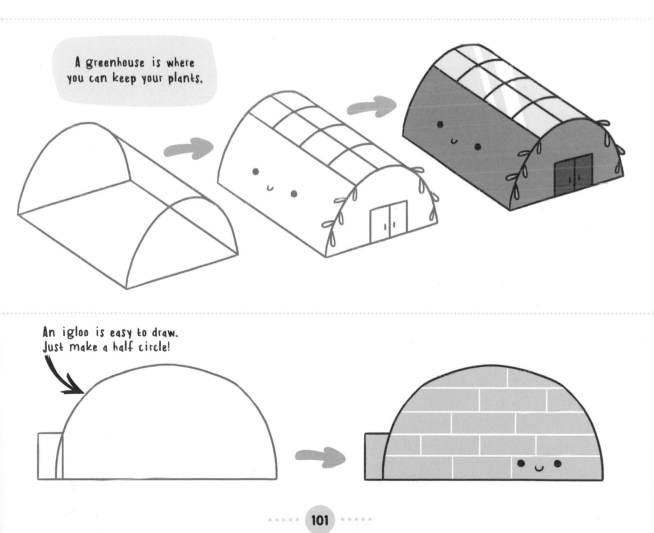

An igloo is easy to draw. Just make a half circle!

SKYSCRAPER

A skyscraper is a very tall building. It can simply be drawn with a long rectangle.

You can make this skyscraper by drawing more than one rectangle.

Some skyscrapers are pointier than others!

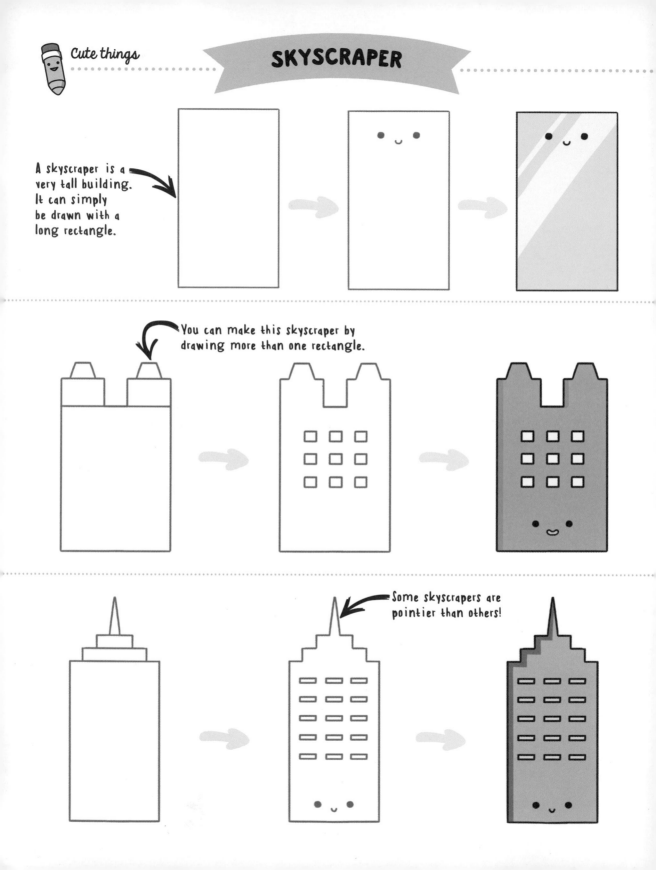

Skyscraper ♥ Tent

Tents are fun for outdoor camping. And indoor camping!

A tepee is just a triangle.

You can add more triangles to make a pattern.

The door of this tent looks like a mouth.

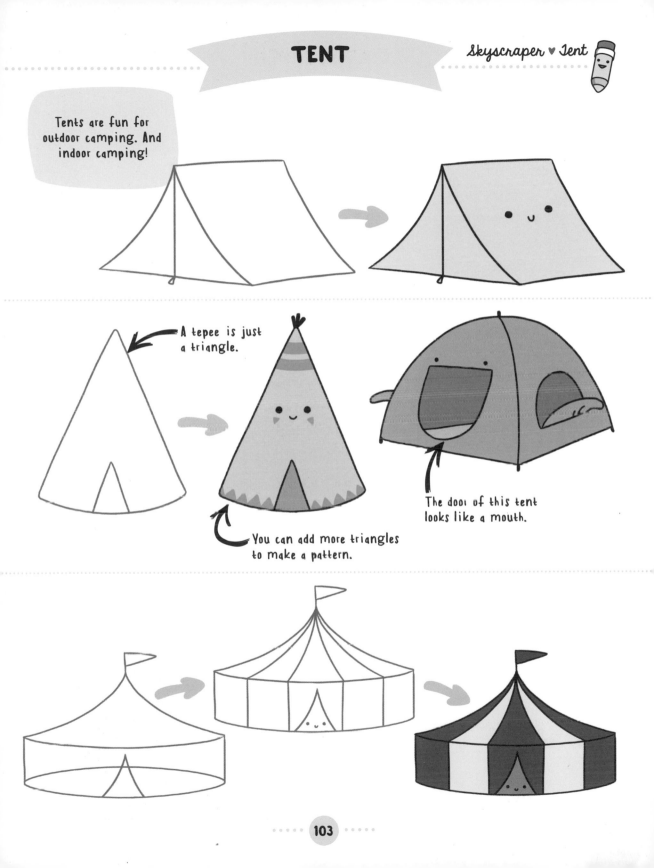

CHAIRS

Give the sofa some pillow friends by drawing squares.

A sofa chair is like the sofa cut in half.

Make the bottom curved so the chair can rock.

Decoration on a table can make it look more fancy.

Tables can have faces on the top or side.

The face of this table is on the side!

Add clothing to your table to give it some personality.

COOKING TOOLS

Most cooking tools have long handles.

Oh no, I'm melting!

The fatter you make the bag, the more icing it has!

Measuring cups come in families.

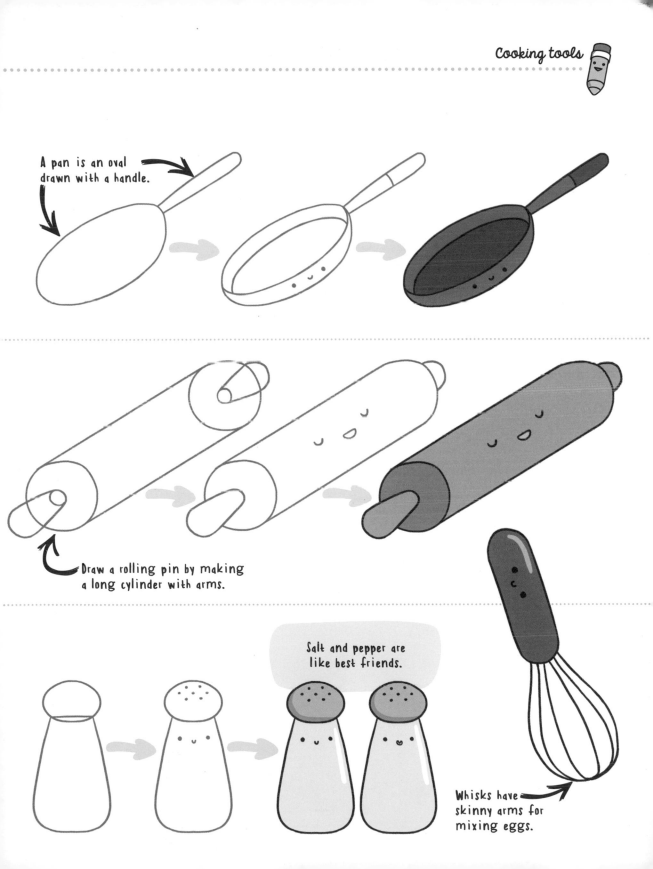

A pan is an oval drawn with a handle.

Draw a rolling pin by making a long cylinder with arms.

Salt and pepper are like best friends.

Whisks have skinny arms for mixing eggs.

VEHICLES

Vroom vroom!

Here's a profile of a car.

You can draw a vehicle's face on the window.

Trucks have more room in the back. You can draw something for it to carry.

You only need to draw two wheels to make a motor bike.

There are many ways to personify a vehicle. This tank's cannon is its nose.

AIR VEHICLES

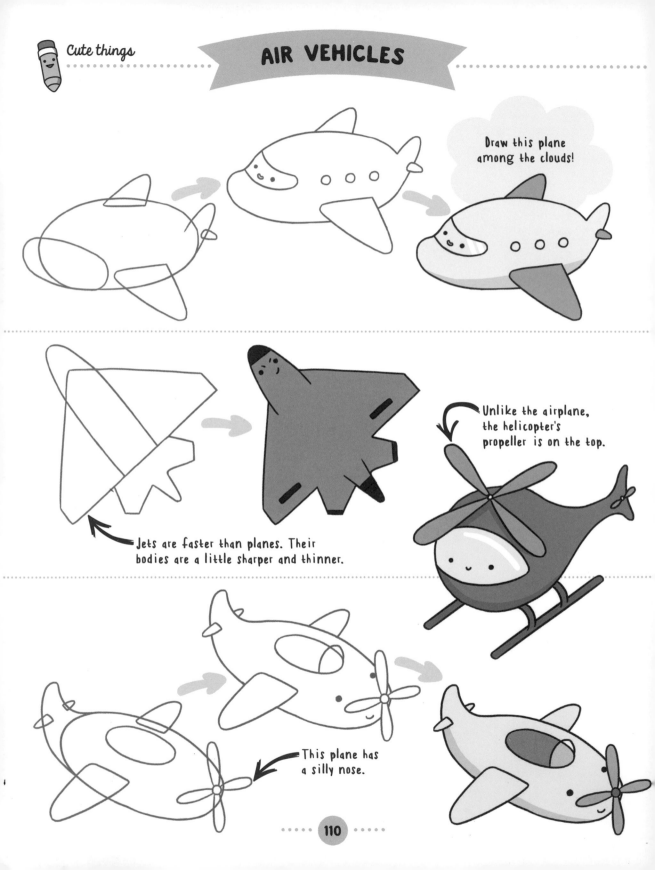

Draw this plane among the clouds!

Jets are faster than planes. Their bodies are a little sharper and thinner.

Unlike the airplane, the helicopter's propeller is on the top.

This plane has a silly nose.

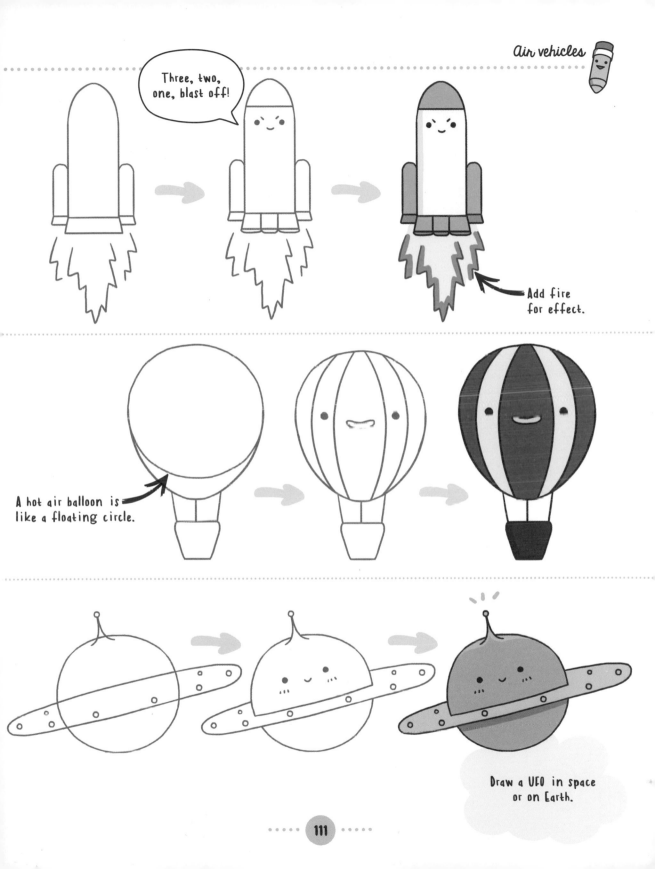

Three, two, one, blast off!

Add fire for effect.

A hot air balloon is like a floating circle.

Draw a UFO in space or on Earth.

111

WATER VEHICLES

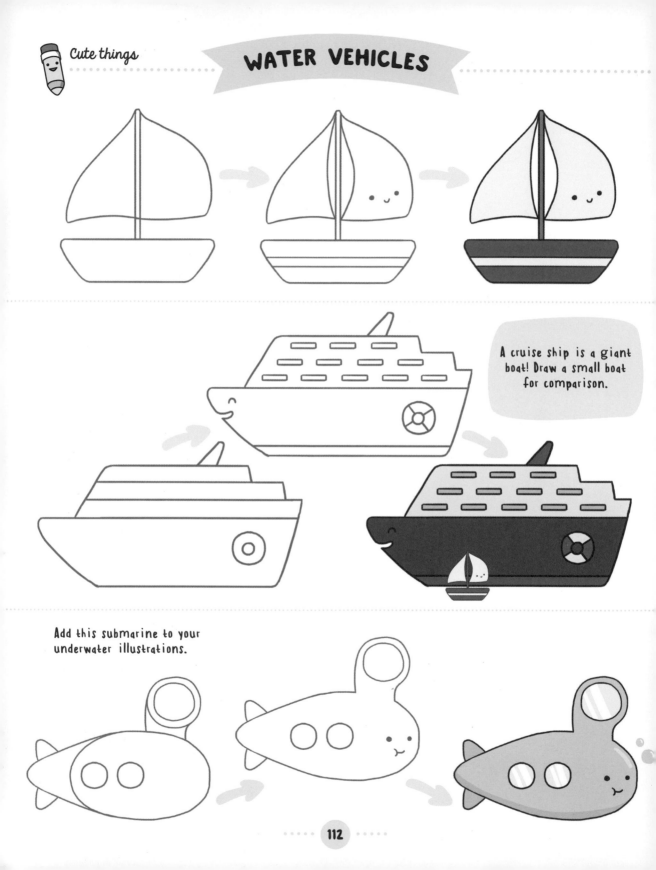

A cruise ship is a giant boat! Draw a small boat for comparison.

Add this submarine to your underwater illustrations.

The front of a jet ski comes to a point. This helps it move faster on water.

Every kayak needs its paddles.

A kayak is a small, narrow boat that can fit one or two passengers on board.

A raft also has paddles, but its body is a lot rounder.

BOWL

Alphabet soup! Try spelling your name in this bowl.

Noodles are like a pattern. Add repeating lines to draw them.

Noodles can be drawn to look like hair.

Make your salad even more colorful by adding nuts or fruit.

Instead of drawing a face on the bowl, try drawing it on the food.

BREAD

Baguettes can be large or small.

These bread buns are like bundles of circles.

Draw a puddle around the butter to make it melt on the toast.

Bread is usually bought in loaves like this.

COTTON CANDY

Draw three wide ovals for the body of your cotton candy.

Draw a larger, more exaggerated triangle for cotton candy that is about to be eaten.

Cotton candy comes in all kinds of shapes. Don't be afraid to make it tall!

Choose three cute colors for a bag of cotton candy.

Drawing the face on the stick instead of the body makes the candy look like hair!

PIZZA

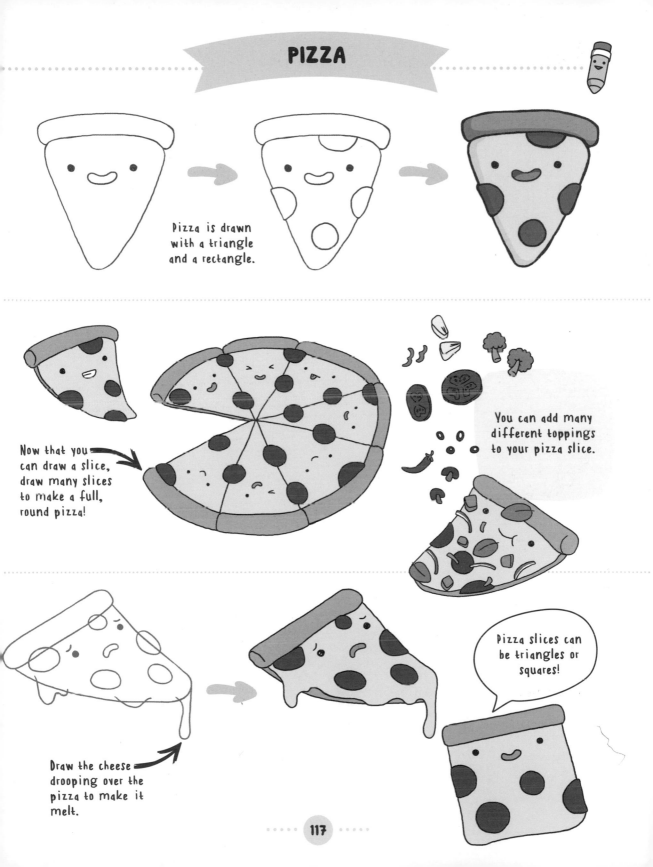

Pizza is drawn with a triangle and a rectangle.

Now that you can draw a slice, draw many slices to make a full, round pizza!

You can add many different toppings to your pizza slice.

Draw the cheese drooping over the pizza to make it melt.

Pizza slices can be triangles or squares!

BURGER

A hamburger has many colors and flavors!

Add a bite mark to the burger to make it look eaten.

There are multiple layers to a burger. Draw what is usually in your burger.

This burger is giving a hug to its french fry friends!

CANDY

Draw many chocolate parts to make chocolate buddies.

Wrapped candy can be drawn with a circle and two triangles.

Color your lollipop with a swirly pattern.

Candy corn is usually eaten during Halloween, but I like to eat it all the time.

Add little white dots to show the sprinkled sugar on gumdrops.

DESSERT

If you'd like to, add more frosting and fruit to the top or side.

Draw ice-cream scoops stacked on top of each other to make them friends.

Donuts have all kinds of toppings. I usually draw sprinkles on mine.

Drawing little hands makes it look like the cupcake is peeking out.

Give this cake a surprised face. It's about to be eaten!

This ice-cream cone has swirly mint hair.

Ice cream can also be eaten in a cup.

Try adding a filling to this pie.

FRUIT

You can color your apple red, yellow, or green.

Oranges are easy to draw. They're just circles!

Make sure not to draw your bananas too round. They will look like moons!

A watermelon slice is a simple triangle.

Look at the detail in this drawing. There are so many strawberry seeds!

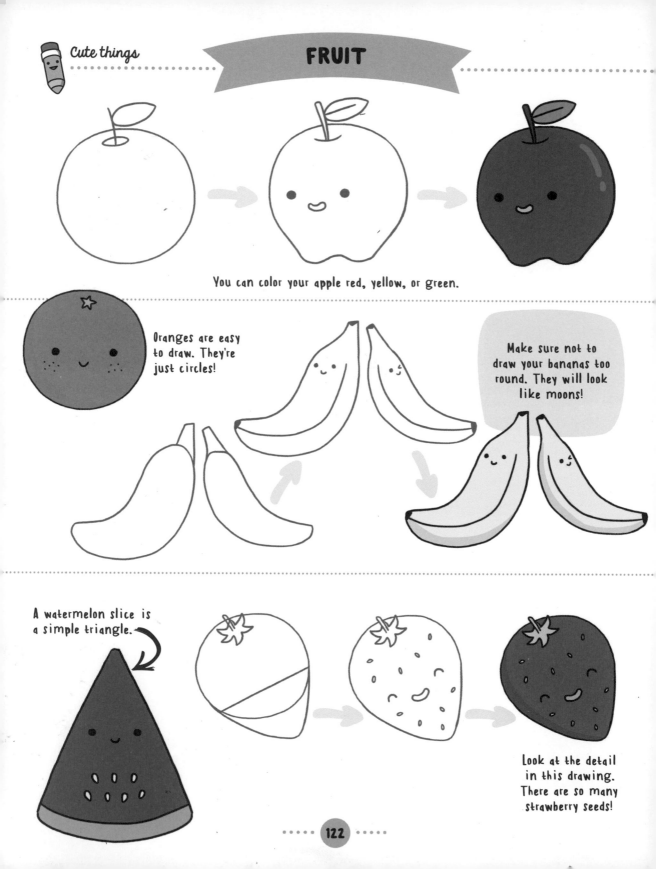

Fruit ♥ Sushi

Sushi have a seaweed wrap and fish or rice filling.

The wrapping on this sushi acts like a shirt.

This sushi is wearing a hat.

The fish looks like a backpack on this sushi.

Some sushi rolls have rice on the outside.

FLOWERS

A sunflower consists of one large circle and small half circles.

Tulips are made of a circle and triangles.

There are so many different types of flowers. The lily has an interesting shape.

Draw many flowers wrapped together to create a bouquet! Choose different kinds of flowers and make your bouquet unique.

Roses are red, violets are blue, this rose can be drawn by you!

HANGING PLANTS

Some plants hang from the ceiling!

Vines likes to hang from above. They also like to wrap around other objects.

This hanging plant has a clear container.

Plants don't always need a container. This plant is naked! You can see its little roots.

Hanging plants can outgrow their pots. The leaves of this plant even cover the pot!

TREES

Drawing a tree is like drawing a fuzzy lollipop. It's just a circle with a stem.

The shape and color of the tree's head can change its personality.

Without the leaves, the tree just looks like this log! Nothing wrong with a log, but leaves are so important when drawing trees.

This tree has hanging leaves.

A pine tree is a big green triangle.

Add little lines to this cactus to make it look prickly.

Draw sunglasses on this palm tree and it will instantly be ready for vacation.

AUTHOR ACKNOWLEDGEMENTS

I want to thank my roommate, Jenny, for taking care of me during this cute adventure. Thanks for letting me use your room sometimes as a workspace, and reminding me to eat. And a big thanks to my little sister, Noodle, for helping me choose illustration colors. I hope it was more fun than it was work!

CREDITS

Quarto would like to thank the following agencies for supplying images for inclusion in this book: Wilkins, Phil, p.10; Shutterstock/Africa Studio, p.11t; Shutterstock/PhuShutter, p.11m; Shutterstock/s_oleg website, p.11b.

QUAR.DCUT

Editor: Kate Burkett
Senior art editor: Emma Clayton
Designer: Karin Skanberg
Art director: Caroline Guest
Creative director: Moira Clinch
Publisher: Samantha Warrington